Emanuele
d'Astorga

Stabat Mater

Edited by Robert King

vocal score

MUSIC DEPARTMENT

OXFORD
UNIVERSITY PRESS

T0088423

OXFORD
UNIVERSITY PRESS

Great Clarendon Street, Oxford OX2 6DP,
United Kingdom

Oxford University Press is a department of the University of Oxford.
It furthers the University's objective of excellence in research, scholarship,
and education by publishing worldwide. Oxford is a registered trade mark of
Oxford University Press in the UK and in certain other countries

First published 2012

Impression: 1

ISBN 978–0–19–338815–4

Music originated in Sibelius
Printed in Great Britain on acid-free paper by
Halstan & Co. Ltd, Amersham, Bucks.

The orchestral score and parts are available on hire/rental
from the publisher's hire library.

Scoring: SATB soloists, SATB chorus,
vln 1, vln 2, vla, vc, cb, organ, and optional theorbo

Duration: c.27 minutes

PREFACE

Emanuele d'Astorga (1680–?1757) was one of the most colourful figures in early eighteenth-century music, and his biography has been shrouded by the legends that were invented after his death. Like Boccherini, Astorga lived and worked in both Spain and Italy. Although his family was of Spanish descent, they acquired a Sicilian barony in the early seventeenth century, living first in Augusta and then, after an earthquake in 1693, in Palermo. While Emanuele was a teenager his father was banished from Palermo after attempting to murder Emanuele's mother, forfeiting his noble title to his eldest son. Subsequently nobility and rights were restored, and the father was elected a senator of the city. Emanuele was, as his family status might suggest, well-educated, and he showed considerable early talent in music, writing an opera at the age of eighteen. But he seems also to have inherited his father's hot temper, leaving home after a quarrel early in his twenties and eventually settling in Rome. There he became associated with the circle of Spain's papal ambassador, the Duke of Osseda, becoming friends with poets such as the Neapolitan Sebastiano Biancardi, who soon became Astorga's principal librettist. On a visit to Genoa the two men were robbed by their servant, and to raise funds they wrote an opera, *Dafni*, of which only the first Act survives.

In the audience at *Dafni*'s first performance in Genoa in April 1709 was Charles III, the Habsburg claimant to the Spanish throne. Much impressed by the music he had heard, he quickly summoned Astorga to his court at Barcelona. When Charles became Emperor, Astorga moved with the court to Vienna, where he had been granted a large pension. The Venetian composer Antonio Caldara was also working in Vienna at the time, and Astorga became godfather to one of his daughters. He also ran up some large debts, which may have contributed to his sudden departure from Austria in 1714. By siding with the Austrians during the War of the Spanish Succession, Astorga forfeited the estates and title that he would have inherited from his father (his brother also having died), but these were reclaimed and made over to him by his mother and sister. Marrying a fifteen-year-old girl in 1717, Emanuele lived for another four years in Sicily. He had three daughters, who he deserted, and moved to Lisbon, never to return to his family or homeland. The remainder of Emanuele's life is a mystery; there are unconfirmed reports (from the often embroidering pen of the eighteenth-century English historian John Hawkins) that Astorga 'passed a winter or two in London, from where he went to Bohemia', but little else is known. His last manuscript is dated 1731, and by 1744 the family estates in Sicily had been sold by his wife and sister, now heavily in debt.

In his day, Astorga was best known for his chamber cantatas, of which more than 150 survive. These are well written and tuneful, and were thoroughly popular. But by far and away his most enduring work proved to be a setting of the *Stabat Mater*, his only surviving sacred work. The piece appeared in many manuscript copies and was published several times, being performed with considerable frequency. Whether attracted by the apparent romance of his adventurous life or by the allure of a wild nobleman who wrote good music, a veritable cult for Astorga grew up during the nineteenth century. Epics, dramas, and novellas were written about the composer and, in the absence of much fact, legends were invented, colourfully describing the gruesome death of his father on the scaffold. In 1866 Johann Joseph Abert wrote an opera in which Astorga becomes deranged, only being brought back to sanity when his wife plays a few bars of his *Stabat Mater* setting.

Throughout the *Stabat Mater* we see Astorga's gift for writing warm melodies that are typical of the Neapolitan style of the time. He also captures the melancholy of this most desolate of sacred texts and, especially in the choruses, demonstrates a thorough grasp of counterpoint, though never at the expense of musicality. In his scoring, Astorga takes a variety of combinations of chorus, solo, duet, and trio. The *Stabat Mater* demonstrates an enormously attractive musical style, featuring a mixture of melody with melancholy, sweetness tempered with mild chromaticism, old-fashioned polyphony contrasted with Neapolitan cantilena, a surprisingly Germanic use of motivic development in the bel canto bass solo movement, and a final, quietly operatic chorus that gently directs the listener away from the Virgin's sorrow towards the Carmelite missal's more optimistic 'palm of victory'. Composers and their work often enjoy a bumpy progression through history, but few paths can have been as bizarre as that of Astorga: in the eighteenth century a musical nobleman, during the nineteenth century a folk hero, and in the twentieth and twenty-first centuries a figure that has fallen into near oblivion.

ROBERT KING
Suffolk, 2012

Editorial practice

As with other editions in the *Classic Choral Works* series, the aim is first and foremost to serve the practical needs of non-specialist choirs, keeping the music pages as clean and uncluttered as possible, though not neglecting the needs of the scholar. Barring has been shown in a modern, standard way; time and key signatures have been modernized. Capitalization within the text has been made consistent to take account of the original line commencements. Errors in the source that have been corrected are listed in this commentary. All material in square brackets or in small print is editorial. Full-size accidentals are those that appear in the source; they are silently omitted when made unnecessary by a modern key signature, and also omitted for immediate repetitions of the same note in the same bar. Small accidentals are editorial. Cautionary accidentals are shown full size in round brackets. Beaming and stemming of notes has been modernized.

A keyboard part has been created in a playable form, without indicating every element of movement within individual polyphonic voices, especially where these cross. This sometimes results in apparent parallel fifths and octaves, but this is surely preferable to the frequent sight of upstems and downstems crossed. Where all the voices are impossible to play, the keyboard reduction has been discreetly simplified. In the continuo-only sections, an editorial continuo realization has been provided.

The work can be performed with an accompaniment of string quartet, ideally with the addition of a sixteen-foot string bass, or with a small string orchestra. In either case, the continuo section should certainly contain chamber organ and, if possible, a theorbo.

Source and variants

Notes

1. Specific references to musical notes in the score are given thus: bar number (Arabic), stave number counting down from top stave in each system (Roman), symbol number in the bar (Arabic).

2. Only variants relevant to vocal lines are listed below; a more comprehensive commentary is available in the full score available on hire/rental from the publisher.

Primary source: British Library R.M.22.a.8 [RM]. Also consulted: BL Egerton MS 2458 [Eg.] and BL Add 5049 [Add.]. *Method*: While there are few disparities in notes and ficta between the three sources consulted, underlay shows more variety. In general, underlay indicated in the primary source has been followed, but where a more natural underlay in one of the additional sources is briefly preferable, this has been incorporated.

Variants

Mvt 1: 22 i 4: source erroneously gives ♭, clashing with tenor / 51 iv 1–5 & 53 iii 1–5: text underlay from Eg. preferred / 57 i 2: source places text syllable one note earlier, though not in similar subsequent phrases

Mvt 2: original time signature 𝄵

Mvt 3: 73 ii 2–74 ii 3: ill-fitting underlay, replaced by that in Eg.

Mvt 4: original time signature ¢ / 48 ii 2: RM shows e♮ against ♭ in bass, corrected by reference to both Eg. and Add. / 111 iv 2: source gives f, but g in basso continuo, here preferred

Mvt 5: original time signature 𝄵

Mvt 6: tempo indication taken from Eg. / 30 ii 2: tie missing in source

Mvt 7: original time signature 𝄵 / 14 iv 2: source gives e, but f in continuo, here preferred

Mvt 8: tempo in RM marked 'Poco andantino'. Eg. gives 'Poco andante', here preferred / 68 i 1: source adds a trill, not shown in Add.

Mvt 9: original time signature 𝄵 / 63 i 2: tie is editorial / 105: fermata editorial in all parts.

Stabat Mater

13th-century Latin Hymn
?Jacopone da Todi (*c*.1230–?1306)

1. Stabat Mater
(Chorus)

EMANUELE D'ASTORGA
(1680–?1757)
edited by Robert King

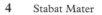

Juxta crucem, sta - bat Ma - ter do - lo - ro - sa jux-
-lo - ro - sa Juxta cru - cem, sta - bat Ma - ter,
Sta - bat Ma - ter do - lo - ro - sa
-ro - sa Juxta cru - cem,   jux - ta

- ta cru - cem la - cry-mo - sa, Dum pen - de
juxta cru - cem la - cry-mo-sa, Dum pen - de
Juxta cru - cem la - cry-mo - sa, Dum pen - de
cru - cem, juxta cru - cem la - cry-mo-sa, Dum pen - de - bat, dum

gla - - - - di -us.

gla - - - di - us.

gla - - di - us.

gla - - - di - us.

2. O quam tristis et afflicta
(Trio: soprano, tenor, & bass)

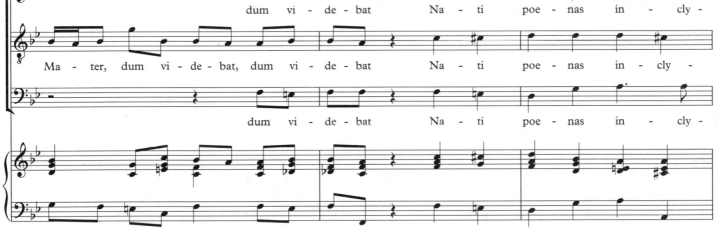

-le -bat, Pi - a Ma -ter, dum vi - de -bat, vi -

-re -bat et do -le -bat, Pi - a Ma -ter dum vi -de -bat, vi -

moe -re - bat et do -le -bat, dum vi - de -bat, vi -

-de -bat Na - ti poe -nas in -cly -ti.

-de -bat Na -ti poe -nas in -cly -ti.

-de -bat Na - ti poe -nas in -cly -ti.

3. Quis est homo
(Duets for soprano & alto, and tenor & bass)

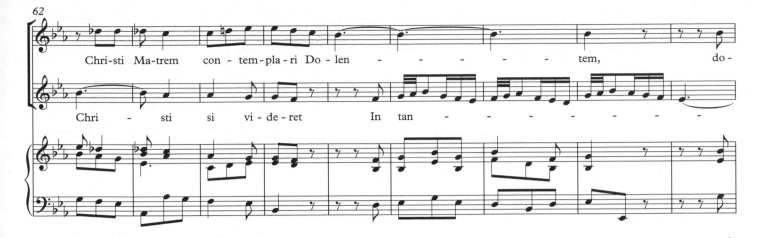

Chri-sti Ma-trem con-tem-pla-ri Do-len - - - - tem, do-

Chri - sti si vi - de - ret In tan -

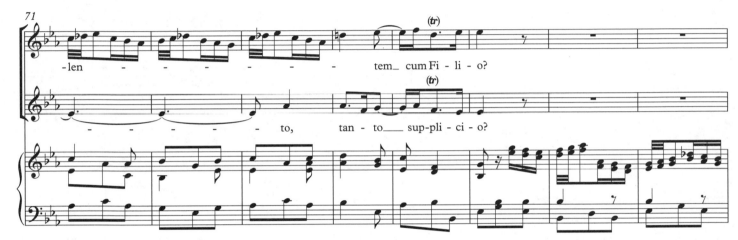

-len - - - - - tem cum Fi - li - o?

- - - - to, tan - to sup-pli - ci - o?

TENOR SOLO

T.

Pro pec - ca - tis su - o gen-tis Vi-dit

T.

Je - sum in tor - men-tis, Et fla - - - - gel - lis sub - di - tum.

BASS SOLO

B.

Vi-dit

su-um dul-cem Na -tum Mo - ri -en-do de - so - la - - - - tum,

- - tum, Dum e - mi - sit spi - ri -tum.

TENOR SOLO

Pro pec - ca - tis su-o gen -tis Vi - dit Je - sum in tor-men - tis, Et fla- gel -

BASS SOLO

Vi - dit su- um dul-cem Na -tum Mo - ri - en - do de-so - la -tum, Dum e-

- - lis, et fla- gel - - - - lis sub - di -tum.

- mi - sit, e - mi-sit spi - ri - tum.

4. Eia Mater
(Chorus)

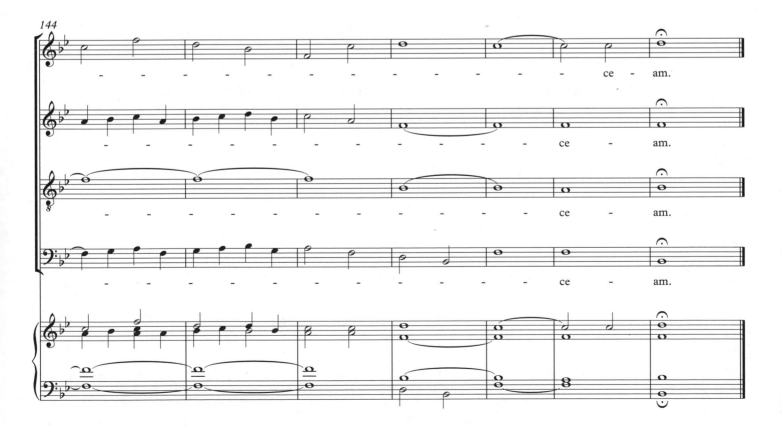

5. Sancta Mater
(Soprano solo)

San-cta Ma - ter, i-stud a - gas, Cru-ci - fi - xi fi - ge pla - gas Cor-de

me - o, cor-de me - o va - li - de, cru-ci - fi - xi, cru-ci - fi - xi fi - ge pla - gas, san-cta

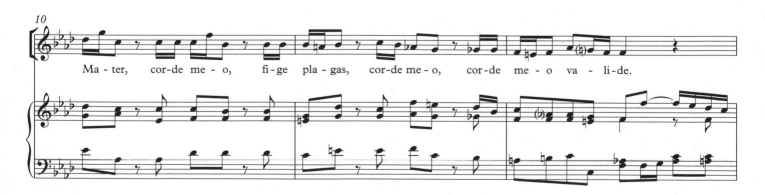

Ma - ter, cor-de me - o, fi - ge pla - gas, cor-de me - o, cor-de me - o va - li - de.

Tu - i Na - ti vul - ne - ra - ti, vul - ne-

-ra - ti, Tam di-gna - ti pro me pa - ti, pro me pa- ti, Poe - nas me - cum di - vi-de. Tu - i

Na - ti vul - ne - ra - ti, Tam dig - na - ti, pro me pa - ti, Poe - nas me-cum, poe - nas me - cum di - vi-

-de, poe - nas me-cum, poe - nas me - cum di - vi-de.

6. Fac me tecum pie flere
(Alto & tenor duet)

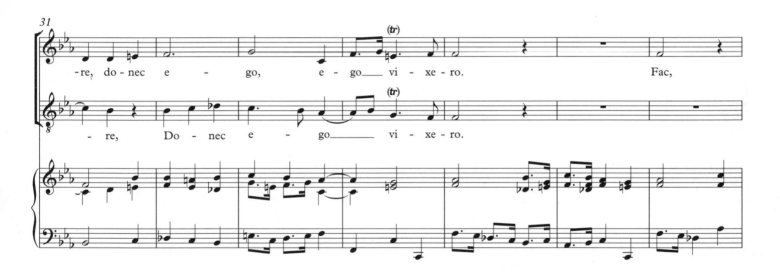

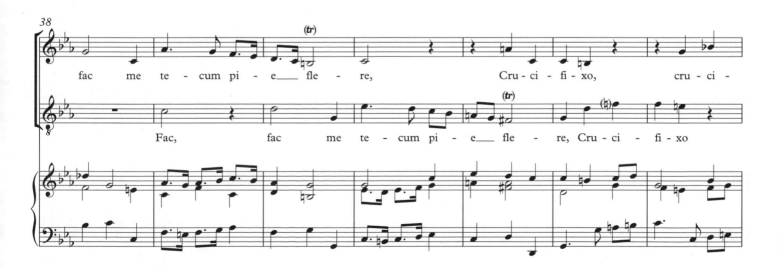

7. Virgo virginum praeclara
(Chorus)

36

8. Fac me plagis vulnerari
(Bass solo)

9. Christe, quum sit hinc exire
(Chorus)